The Outlaw James Copeland and the Champion-Belted Empress

The Outlaw James Copeland and the Champion-Belted Empress

Poems by

Jeanne Lebow

The University of Georgia Press
Athens and London

Published by the University of Georgia Press
Athens, Georgia 30602

Set in Ehrhardt with Gill Sans Bold display
The paper in this book meets the guidelines
for permanence and durability of the
Committee on Production Guidelines for
Book Longevity of the Council on
Library Resources.

Printed in the United States of America

95 94 93 92 91 5 4 3 2 1

Library of Congress Cataloging in
Publication Data

Lebow, Jeanne.
The outlaw James Copeland and the
champion-belted empress : poems / by
Jeanne Lebow.
p. cm.
ISBN 0-8203-1280-0 (alk. paper).—ISBN
0-8203-1281-9 (pbk. : alk. paper)
I. Title.
PS3562.E26485O9 1991
811′.54—dc20 90-36868
CIP

British Library Cataloging in Publication Data
available

for Steve

Acknowledgments

I wish to express my gratitude to Bin Ramke, Carolyn Forché, and Sallie Anderson for their faith in my work. Thanks also go to Angela Ball, D. C. Berry, Kim Herzinger, David Roberts, Maureen Ryan, Kenneth Watson, and the staff at the University of Georgia Press for their assistance and encouragement during various stages in the preparation of this manuscript.

A special thanks goes to my husband Steve Shepard, who introduced me to the story of James Copeland, to my family, and to the families of writers at Northeast Missouri State University, the University of Ouagadougou, the University of Southern Mississippi, Memphis State University, and Hollins College.

In addition, I want to acknowledge the support magazine editors give to poets and poetry. These poems, sometimes in earlier versions, appeared in the following publications:

Caesura: "Counterpane"
A Carolina Literary Companion: "Mockingbird"
Chariton Review: "Witnesses: Copeland's Last Tale"
Memphis State Review: "Fish Fry" (first appeared with the title "Emma")
New Virginia Review: "Trade Wind Hotel"
Nimrod: "Field Peas," "Reticulation," "Running Feet"
Poems from the Earth: On Nature & the Environment: "Cutting In"
Product 6: "Waiting"
South Florida Poetry Review: "The Blues Are Red and Green," "Flush Times," "Pulling Down the Tomatoes," "Skin the Deer to Cool the Meat"

Contents

The Island

Epilogue

". . . herein we see the rare virtue of a strong individual vitality, and the rare virtue of thick walls, and the rare virtue of interior spaciousness. Oh, man! admire and model thyself after the whale! Do thou, too, live in this world without being of it. Be cool at the equator; keep thy blood fluid at the Pole. Like the great dome of St. Peter's, and like the great whale, retain, O man! in all seasons a temperature of thine own."

Herman Melville, *Moby Dick* (1851)

Prologue

Needle Picture

With cheerful mind we yield to men
The higher honors of the pen
The needle's our great care
In this we chiefly wish to shine
How far the art's already mine
This sampler does declare.

Sampler, 1817

African women drew
threads through their teeth
and speech began.
A woman's mouth—
language and the loom.
Yet men say a black
woman has no right
to weave herself

a story, no right to be
a One and Only Hero and Bareback
Champion-Belted Empress.
They cut the threads
of my words and push
the string of their
song into my throat.
For me they weave

the long red dust.
Three basins of water
can't wash
my face or cool
the sting of sun and flies.
And with rain, hems

dragging mud, feet
never dry.

For themselves they weave
the top shine of the circus.
Each man straddles two horses
while other horses with flags
pass between his legs.
The men throw off their Roman
capes and helmets and somersault
to the ground, then vault

onto the flagged backs.
One woman, an equilibrist
in soft slippers, balances
on a slackwire, her parasol in hand.
Then she climbs to the big top
and swings from a bar. A man
with a moustache pushes
forward to catch her.

He gets the applause.
She fans her face, waves
an ostrich plume at the crowd.
Then she goes back to her needle
and embroiders men's stories.
She pins up her skirts
so the cloth does not drag.
But me, I break right past

that shooter to thick quilts,
to sand and water
packed like batting
between pieced layers, flannel
beneath, shifting

fins and wings above.
And waves coming in
on the bias, seaming

the mantles, big rollers
pressing each edge.
I go where a border of sargassum
weed floats over eelgrass,
where stingrays school
and flap across one quilt field.
Where jack-a-dandies, their yellow
tails bursting through the swells,

button down the mullet
straight through the center squares.
Here rings of black and white and red
radiate from the lagoon's eye:
blackbirds, skimmers.
Beached jellyfish—violet
and pink—bubble along one hem,
prickly pear flowers along another.

Here light pierces
the parts, knots
surface and center.
And I am apart from women who
swim like ballyhoo onto grassbeds
and hover: a paper of pins,
their noses pointed one way.
I will not shut my mouth.

I file my teeth, sharpen
the points of my loom,
and recall
the origin of language.

Pinelands

Cockfight

First out, yellow jackets
swarm over the snapped pines, over
a red oak uprooted near our well.
The hens scratch, herding
their chicks back
and forth among the leaf litter.
But no cocks crow.
Uncle runs to his pens now,
pens smashed by the trees.
Red, orange, black, the ruffs
fluff up toward the combs.
Not one cock alive, and only
one rooster killed by a limb.

Uncle pokes each bird
with a cane knife, points out
torn muscles, slashes, stabs.
Wind brought down the coops
but not these birds, he says.
Freed up, they
moved on each other, beating
their wings for height
and sinking their spurs
deep into other necks and chests.
They raked each other
to the ground, drove
their beaks in for the kill.

I watch Uncle crop each foot
and sharpen the spur: straight
razors for more pit birds.

Fish Fry

A mess of bream.
Mama feeds the cats
threads of intestines,
drops the fish
tails first into the grease.
Three more passes of the knife:
a lemon falls
into quarters.
She squeezes a crescent, lets
the juice run over
her arms, her palms.
The dipper rinses
fish scales and lemon pulp
into the basin, leaving
only the scent of citrus on skin.

Field Peas

Any fool knows you can't
curtsy with your lap
full of field peas.
But he slinks
round the corner
with his wink and howdy,
and I jump up
like a hen, startling
those peas down the steps.
He laughs, says a woman
pretty as me shouldn't
trouble herself with peas.

Next day he is taking
breakfast off Mrs. Dorothy's Haviland,
sweet-mouthing how I ought to be
fed with a silver spoon,
not be the one polishing.
Then he wraps the blue silk
he sold Mrs. Dorothy
round and round my waist, reaches
into the greens I'm rinsing, holds
my hands under his.
Can't stand
to move on without you, Mary.

Two nights later I leave
Mama's kitchen, grab
hold of a mare's halter.
Girl, I better never catch you

galloping after no trash.
Mama's hope scatters
like a mess of peas.

Testing the Lord

Child, don't you know
how the lizard got flat?
Testing the Lord, child.
Testing the good Lord.
Frog says Lord spare me
a squeeze through this crack.
But Lizard says Lord
or no Lord I'll get through.
And that log comes
right down, smashes him
flat as a Bible page.
So unless you prefers
crawling on your belly
the rest of your born days
don't act like no lizard.

Mockingbird

God let death
slip into the world
but sent women
new skins to protect them—
Jacob's coats, rainbow-colored.
Mama tells how a snake
bit the messenger and stole
the basket of skins.
And every spring now the snake
chooses a different skin, admires
himself in the glass.

When I was five, I hunted
that basket, expecting
to come upon it
like Moses in the bullrushes.
Instead I saw
a mockingbird dancing for a snake.
The bird hopped. The moccasin
followed, its movement
thick and mottle-bellied.
The snake lunged,
the bird flew into a live oak.

Mama broke
her hoe across the moccasin's back.
The snake
tried to slide away, but Mama
stepped behind it, raked
its head across the ground.
The cottonmouth slung

its shot of venom
high against the oak's trunk,
curled off to shed
his old skin for a fresh one.

Savanna

The soil here doesn't hold
water: water holds
the soil, allows silt
enough for crawdad mounds.

Palmetto, rattlesnakes, cranes
fatten here. Face to face
the birds leap,
bow their red foreheads

and leap again. Bow
and leap. The bog fills
with green buttercups, each
hanging among rows

of long-neck jugs. Small flies
drop into these green pitchers
and dissolve in the water.

The Great Fire: Copeland's First Tale

Mobile, 1839

Those fancy dry goods?
Yeah, Mary. The genteel
life's for me.
Brother Wages and I
we reconnoitered
that stuff I sold
your Mrs. Dorothy.
Five thousand worth:
all muslin and silk.
That night we brought
dark lanterns and picked out
cloth, swept through
the pocket watches,
our false key
unlocking the doors.
Men packed the goods
on butcher carts, rolled
them to the boats.
Our guards
shifted off at midnight,
so we kindled
every store we robbed.
The wind blowing with us,
we looted shop
after shop, piled
liquor and meat
onto the carts, then hopped
the boats for Dog River.

Mobile sure outshone
the courthouse fire

I set in Jackson County.
Flames topped
the tallest pines.
And this haul beat stealing
pigs and pretty penknives.

Flush Times

He waves a palmetto leaf,
a bright hand
across my face, declares himself
this man Anthony and me
Queen of the Nile.
He calls that Cleopatra
a likely woman.

The new green of cypress
rushes the banks, the knees
jogging the horses
blowing in the river.
Grapes and honeysuckle
open to the day, the vines
stretching toward our pirogue.

Peppers—red and green.
Biscuits, dried beef,
cheese. A filched
pie from Mrs. Dorothy's pantry.
Possum and turkey roasting.
A two-headed gourd
full of cognac.

A palmetto clump stirs,
a yellow and lilac whip
lacing up the stems.
I finger the jewels
chaining my neck.
Back then he didn't say
nothing about Cleopatra's snake.

Skin the Deer to Cool the Meat

I pull my hand
back from the insides,
spread the heart
flat on a swamp magnolia leaf
and gut the buck.
With green sticks I stretch the rib cage,
then draw another flint knife
and skin the deer to cool the meat.

I study the pouch of points, finger
the shaft no longer flagging its mark.
And I remember hunting with my brother.
That day his bow brought down a deer.
To celebrate, we carved suns on our forearms.
Our blades abrading childhood
and sealing our friendship, we
skinned our wrists to leach the spirits.

Now I take clams from my waist thong,
crush pokeberries and splay a sassafras root.
Then purpling this brush, I encircle
a circle on the smooth-trunked bull bay
and cross a line with another inside the rings,
claiming a point for each wind, for each hoof.
I crown the painted sun with a rack of red antlers
and skin the bark to mingle the saps.

Picking It Out

Picking It Out

Cotton bursts them bolls
but it don't sit up high
like no dewberry you can pluck
without paining your fingers.

Seems like your husband-to-be
would hatch some better plan
than his woman be dragging
a canvas sack in the red dirt

and her never worked
nowhere but her mama's kitchen.
Girl, Sister said, get yourself
up to the house. You can wait

right smart up there, stead of
spoiling in the field.
Cook and sew. Live with
okra, not that cotton.

Waiting

Two king snakes jump
from the wash into my arms.

I stand here like that sign
in the doctor's office:
that board with wings and snakes.

One on each arm, the snakes
tighten. I tempt them
loose with saucers of milk.
Yet habit draws them back.

Sister says I look calm.
But she doesn't see the snakes.

Railroad Steel

His mother ate rats
her whole lying-in
to make such a thief.
That man got
a heart like railroad steel.
No auction block.
He'd rather sell me
behind my own rubbed back.
No eyes to meet.
A likely high yellow
always fetches a thousand dollars:
New Orleans Bank bills
and five-dollar gold pieces.

The Christmas Camp Meeting: Copeland's Second Tale

Winter 1841–42

He was a great sinner,
a sinner in his early days.
But the Lord
called him to preach,
called him to save.
Now everyone in Natchitoches
breathes a private
prayer with Brother McGrath.
I trained him myself
in that long Methodist groan
and amen, put out handbills,
even stole his horse
so he could pass the hat
and get another.

With McGrath approaching
the mercy seat, Brother Wages
launched a peddling boat
and converted free Cincinnati blacks
with calico and the notion
we were abolitionists
come to rescue Red River slaves
testifying at McGrath's meeting.
Those slaves sold their crops,
their chickens, brought
their hope of freedom
folded inside their bedrolls.

The free blacks carried
them to us, a wagonload.

Then one of our men acted
the part of a U.S. marshal
ready to haul us all to jail.
He demanded the free blacks
stand trial
or be sold for life.
They chose slavery.
Afterward, Brother McGrath
stripped off
his Methodist coat,
his last amen
and dove into canebrake.
He disguised himself in green
goggles and met us in Vicksburg.

Praise the Lord!
He brought us twenty-five grand—
reselling stolen horses, goods, and men.

The Pond: Uncle's Tale

She pushes through grass
full of crickets, then
heads for the center,
waving to Slider
sunning on his log.
Sister Goose preens
her wings and swims
once around the pond

before Brer Fox arrests
her. No trespassing!
That means you.
But Sister knows her rights.
She takes that fox to court and finds
the sheriff is a fox,
each attorney is a fox,
the jurymen are foxes,

and the judge is a fox.
They try Sister Goose, slit
her throat, and string
her up to let the blood.
Then they roast her.
The little ones
chew on the bones.

Running Feet

The judge had his way
with her, then decided
he'd had enough.
But Chloe stood outside,
her ear to the door.
Eavesdropper, the judge yelled
and sliced off
her left ear.

For the judge's daughter's party
Chloe baked a birthday cake
full of oleander flowers.
The girl died.
So did her mother and sister.
The other slaves dragged
Chloe to the bank of the Mississippi,
lynched her, then dropped

her body in the river.
Trouble if you do,
trouble if you don't
say no.
Chloe, how Mama
could scare us with your story,
your ghost in the green headrag.
Watch me

steal sand from Copeland's tracks,
mix it with pepper and drop
the grains into Four Thieves Vinegar.
I write his name, floating

a cigar paper in the vinegar,
then cork the bottle with root
and pitch it
headlong into the creek.

Heat before the rain
fills the house with flies.
The squall bends trees, squeezes
water through the shutters.
Searching out a dry spot, roaches
drop over the sills. I place
St. Peter at the front door,
St. Michael at the back.

I feed the saints paradise seeds.
No doubt now
that man'll run himself to death.

Meat Aplenty: A Trickster Tale

When hungry times come, the birds
they stay on the wing: flap, flap.
Brother Gar he hears some hawks turn
together flap, flap, flap
down to the shore to drink.
He swims over, asks Brother Hawk if
he's found food. Yes, some fat hens.
Carry me yonder, Gar pleads.
You in a chicken coop?
But Gar sweet-mouths and Hawk
carries him flap, flap, flap.
Gar sits in the pen, picking up
the pieces the hawks drop.

When the watchman comes, the birds
scatter: flap, flap, flap.
And there sits Gar.
Watchman sings and pockets that fish.
Man, if you like singing,
hear me, says Gar.
Just give me a little puddle
and I'll do you proud.
Gar shakes water over himself, singing

> Heads aplenty, feet aplenty
> flap, flap, flap.
> Hawk give me meat aplenty
> flap, flap, flap.

Dancing along the corn rows, Watchman
calls out: Gar,

you sure can sing.
Put me in a big washtub
and I'll do even better, chuckles Gar.
He rolls once around
the tub, soaks his gills,
spreads his fins,
then belts out

> Heads aplenty, feet aplenty
> flap, flap, flap.
> Hawk give me meat aplenty
> flap, flap, flap.

If you put me alongside the bayou
where I can smell the water,
you'll really hear some singing.
Naw, you'll turn me
to a fool, says the watchman.
Don't put my body in the bayou.
Just touch my tail to water.
So Watchman takes Gar to the bayou
and dances when Gar sings

> Heads aplenty, feet aplenty
> flap, flap, flap.
> Hawk give me meat aplenty
> flap, flap, flap.

Watchman dances so hard
he never looks back.
Gar just wriggles and sings,
wriggles and sings, flips himself,
then swims and sings,
swims and swims

Heads aplenty, feet aplenty
flap, flap, flap.
Hawk give me meat aplenty
flap, flap, flap.

That's why if you want to eat Gar,
never let his tail
touch water, never let him sing.

Horses and Mules: Copeland's Third Tale

Texas, 1841

That overseer drank
our poisoned whiskey.
Then Wages and I stole
his slaves and horses,
traveled a brisk gait
several nights before selling
and setting off on foot again.
We found a ranch near San Antonio.
Horned cattle and horses.
Mules, jacks, and jennies.

The rancher loaned us mounts
to hunt and see the country.
We kept the ranch in venison
and returned with a tale:
gold for delivery.
Thirty horses, thirty mules.
The rancher set out
alongside Brother Wages and me
and an Indian drover, bells
ringing on the five lead mules.

The third day we camped
at a spring and hampered
our horses to graze.
We killed a deer and a prairie hen,
then cleaned our guns,
reloading with large buckshot.
Before dawn we crawled
beside the others, fired

dry grass to see
how they lay.

The old man turned to Wages.
He unloaded
a barrel into the man's forehead.
I pulled the trigger on the Indian,
my muzzle between head and neck.
Slinging the bodies with ropes,
swinging them on poles,
we carried them to a sink hole,
dispatching our companions,
paying for our horses and mules.

I cribbed the massive silver spurs,
the silver stirrups and bridle bits,
the gold sleeve buttons.

Flatboats: Copeland's Fourth Tale

Mississippi River, 1842

A western trader. His boats
loaded up: potatoes,
onions, flour, bulk pork.
And a contract to carry
one hundred barrels of whiskey.
Wages and McGrath advanced
cash to buy the barrels
and our help with delivery.
Past the mouth of the Ohio
we lashed the boats together,
stewed some hot whiskey punch.
I smashed the trader's forehead.
We stripped his body, roped
iron cooking grates
(three hundred pounds)
round his neck, and cast
the man overboard.
With the hatchet, Wages
scraped off NonSuch
and Red Rover, renamed
one boat Tip
and the other Tyler too.

Two Tries for Two Bits

The barker runs up the rungs and
honks the horn on the top step.
Yet his climb looks too easy.

So I focus on the top and bottom
pivots, on the twists that can twirl
the ladder like a hammock.

My turn comes to crawl boot over boot.
But the angled ratline whirls on its axis,
spins me on my back like a turtle,
drops me into the dirt.

I watch the barker balance again, watch him
change a swinging bridge to a steel beam.
He pulls it to him, juke style:
straight-armed and fast.

When he makes the flexible
solid, the tension is everything.

Counterpane: Northern Mississippi

Green threads sprouting through bare patches signal
another lifting of the winding sheet.
As Sister's fingers featherstitch feedsack
squares into circles, the wedding-ring quilt
grows. French knots anchor the center of scraps,
cross-stitches parceling the diamonds.
Beyond ice-hemmed panes, cardinals and doves
sway on forsythia. Swatches of down,

they wait to pluck the sunflower kernels
from the ground's coverlet when the damask
cat stalks off. Tailors: their beaks will thread seed
buttons through snow holes, their feet topstitching
the counterpane, appliquéing inter-
looping pawprints with herringbone hoppings.

Pulling Down the Tomatoes

They wilt from the ground up.
A summer of circus tricks
knocks them out. I fence,
cage, stake, and tie
the vines, pick them clean.
Only a few green pin curls
curve up, their yellow flutes
still open to the bees.

I bake the cakes, stare
out the window at the tomatoes.
It's my turn to leave.
All day I cream butter
and sugar, crack out yolks.
Rags wet with kerosene ring
the table legs, keep ants
away from the cooling layers.

I spread the icings,
shape curlicues and bells.

The Island

Trade Wind Hotel: A Newspaper Story

Isle Dernière, August 1856

The door bursts—stopping the violins.
Her fan drops.
Shoved against the table, she topples
the cups onto the New Orleans bonbons.

The wind peels the roof, blasts the south wall,
raises her starched skirts.
She smacks them down.
But they billow around her again like screams.

The other walls blow,
and she crawls toward the levee.
She dodges boards,
bumps a pole.

Hand over hand up the pole into the rain,
she recognizes the children's whirligig,
grabs the bar twirling above her,
and is swept allemande left.

Everything moves horizontally.
Even her pantalettes
plane out over the water,
over the piecrust of the island.

The wind slows, the water drops.
She droops to the ground, sees breakers
rub the bodies back and forth in the gulf
and fiddler crabs cull the sargassum weed.

Patches of yellow chamomile
the tallest things in sight.

Leaving This Shining Ground

Heaven be April fields,
blue-eyed grass, not cotton.
Hummers gorging huckleberry juice
and thistles, and sheepshead
patrolling the outside beach.

Heaven be sleek black grackles
and redwings singing in cane
ribboned with morning glory,
swamp rose, lilies. In June
green tree frogs fill Heaven.

Heaven be orange and October
yellow. Goldenrod and butterfly weed
above the sand, monarchs
bunching on the clusters,
trumpet creeper edging the woods.

Steal away, steal away,
steal away to Jesus.
Gonna break
right past that shooter.
I'm going home,
Lawd, I'm going home.

Queen Anne's Lace

One tiny purple polka
dot amidst crocheted snow.
Parasol
for a finch.
Bridal canopy
for a field mouse.
Or are you gossamer?
Silk of doubt
spun by a backward-looking spider,
Lot's wife,
centered in salt.

Definition

On her sickbed my aunt
never recognizes her husband,
yet calls to mind how he came courting,
six eggs tied in a new bandanna.

At sunset I watch the orange beaks of skimmers
merge with their black backs.
Two lines of marsh grass dim into one,
then blur into the water, into the oaks.

The sun profiles the far pines, their halo
distinct as the pop of bubbles after a bath.

Glissando

As the tide creeps up the grass,
the marsh snail closes his door
tight against the bay and clings.
Then as the water trails away,
he slides down a tendril, glides
past the salt diamonds
glistering among the strands.

I recall anger pressing
me up the back stairs, step by step.
From the landing I would sweep
down the rail
and out the door.
But I always came back inside,
to the hot climb and the cold slide.

Witnesses: Copeland's Last Tale

Augusta, Mississippi
Execution Day—October 30, 1857

For two dollars I beat
Moffitt's wife with a stick
and torched the house, leaving
her there to burn.
Two people,
that's enough to keep a secret.
And if one is dead,
so much the better.

We ate figs and peaches,
whirled on the Black Creek men
and took one out.
Squally times after. I drew
my piece on a man trying
to arrest me, but he pushed
my gun aside and stabbed me.
They tracked me up by the blood.

Thousands now bring cheese and biscuits,
picnic under the bluff's shrub oak
and pines, hand round lemonade
while the cap pulls
over my face and the drop falls.
Reminds me of the day I stole that heifer,
roasted the hindquarters, then shot
the gathering wolves.

I've always thought I filled a room.
But I once saw

a painting of a woman leaning on a piano,
her bell skirt stretched across the canvas,
while a tiny man in the foreground
begged for favors:
        He Proposing,
        She Undecided.

I left Mary in the fields, sold her
as breed stock. Would she
witness for me now, cry out
        Slack your rope, Hangsman?
More likely she'd tighten the noose,
more likely she'd shout
        I've come to see you
        hanging on a longleaf pine.

Reticulation

He says he's learning to relax,
to hypnotize the fist of himself into long ligaments.
He says he'll slide his indigo scales
past the loops of charmers, of constrictors.

Curious, I snake my body toward his,
eye his slight recoil.
My scars are lessons
that all snakes have their own stretches,
their own hibernations, and that massage
makes black racers
tie themselves into impossible knots.

Parallel, we coil and uncoil,
shedding tight skins at our own pace.

The Blues Are Red and Green

The tide runs through the azaleas.
The mullet are jumping.
A few pause in the branches,
their sides glittering crow's nests
full of tinfoil.

He slides a butter knife
down the guitar neck.
His hands are hummingbirds
darting into the flowers,
fast and slow one speed.

A girl dances with the mullet.
They churn the water like children
shaking jars of fireflies.
Shrimp slide between her toes,
jellyfish glow in the foam.

The music puffs out
like a lizard's red flap,
spills color in the dark,
paint on a beach of stones.

Epilogue

Cutting In

1885

I want to keep the thing stirring,
now that the ice is cracked.

Sojourner Truth,
c. 1881–86

The All-Famous and Gigantic Jumbo
Mighty Lord of All Beasts
and Show of Shows trumpeted
past the New York City gawkers.
Sixteen horses pulled
and two elephants
pushed his wagon.

He had arrived in a garden
over twenty years before,
only to be
sold from Paris to London.
Each day the seven-foot trunk
picked up two hundred pounds of hay,
two bushels of oats, a basket of biscuits,
three quarts of onions, five buckets of water,
and gifts of fruit and whiskey.
Then for $10,000 the Zoological Council
crated and shipped
the Largest Living Quadruped
to P. T. Barnum and America.
The English children cried.

But Jumbo lived up to his billing,
thrilled all gawkers,
toured the continent

in his Palace Special rail car, gave
rides to a million children.
There were Jumbo cigars, Jumbo hats,
Jumbo fans, Jumbo pies, Jumbo stews.

What was the fascination?
The leg of a trotting horse
is a delicate line in motion,
the bend of the fetlock thin and elegant.
But the elephant leg shakes
air and earth with the deliberateness
of a cypress tree crossing a marsh.
His big ears fanning, Jumbo could unload
trains, could put up the big top—pulling
ropes to lift the huge float of canvas.
And Barnum couldn't resist owning
a six-ton Towering Monster.
He loved extremes: fake mermaids
and human nightingales.

Jumbo and the midget elephant Tiny Tim
were walking the tracks after an evening show.
A freight train rounded a curve
and tossed Tiny Tim in a ditch.
When it struck Jumbo, the train stopped.
The mighty head—fifteen feet
from ear tip to ear tip—cracked.

Jumbo died minutes later.
Determined to get his money's worth,
Barnum printed
a pamphlet with pictures of Jumbo
shielding Tiny Tim.

Melville shows how long spades
cut a place for the whaling hook.

Then the crew heaved at the windlass,
spiralizing the blubber, stripping
it like peel from an orange.

Jumbo's skin too was seized, mounted
only six years after boys killed
the first elephant in America.
They had wanted to see
if elephant hide was bulletproof.

Dr. J. R. S. Pitts, the sheriff of Perry County, Mississippi, responsible for Copeland's hanging, published the first edition of *The Life and Confession of the Noted Outlaw James Copeland* in 1858. He was promptly sued for libel, supposedly by members of the Copeland-Wages clan. The governor of Mississippi allowed Pitts to be extradited to Mobile, where he was tried, convicted, and then served time for libel. After this stay in jail, Pitts gave up the life of sheriff, became a doctor, and published the second edition of *The Life and Confession* in 1874. Copeland's sympathizers allegedly stole most copies of these first two editions from store shelves and from warehouses. Pitts published a third edition in 1909, and although most of these texts also disappeared, John Guice, a University of Southern Mississippi historian, discovered a copy and arranged for the University Press of Mississippi to reprint the book in 1980.

The Contemporary Poetry Series

Edited by Paul Zimmer

Dannie Abse, *One-Legged on Ice*
Susan Astor, *Dame*
Gerald Barrax, *An Audience of One*
Tony Connor, *New and Selected Poems*
Franz Douskey, *Rowing Across the Dark*
Lynn Emanuel, *Hotel Fiesta*
John Engels, *Vivaldi in Early Fall*
John Engels, *Weather-Fear: New and Selected Poems, 1958–1982*
Brendan Galvin, *Atlantic Flyway*
Brendan Galvin, *Winter Oysters*
Michael Heffernan, *The Cry of Oliver Hardy*
Michael Heffernan, *To the Wreakers of Havoc*
Conrad Hilberry, *The Moon Seen as a Slice of Pineapple*
X. J. Kennedy, *Cross Ties*
Caroline Knox, *The House Party*
Gary Margolis, *The Day We Still Stand Here*
Michael Pettit, *American Light*
Bin Ramke, *White Monkeys*
J. W. Rivers, *Proud and on My Feet*
Laurie Sheck, *Amaranth*
Myra Sklarew, *The Science of Goodbyes*
Marcia Southwick, *The Night Won't Save Anyone*
Mary Swander, *Succession*
Bruce Weigl, *The Monkey Wars*
Paul Zarzyski, *The Make-Up of Ice*

The Contemporary Poetry Series

Edited by Bin Ramke

J. T. Barbarese, *New Science*
J. T. Barbarese, *Under the Blue Moon*
Scott Cairns, *The Translation of Babel*
Richard Cole, *The Glass Children*
Wayne Dodd, *Echoes of the Unspoken*
Wayne Dodd, *Sometimes Music Rises*
Joseph Duemer, *Customs*
Karen Fish, *The Cedar Canoe*
Caroline Knox, *To Newfoundland*
Patrick Lawler, *A Drowning Man Is Never Tall Enough*
Sydney Lea, *No Sign*
Jeanne Lebow, *The Outlaw James Copeland and the Champion-Belted Empress*
Phillis Levin, *Temples and Fields*
Gary Margolis, *Falling Awake*
Jacqueline Osherow, *Looking for Angels in New York*
Donald Revell, *The Gaza of Winter*
Martha Clare Ronk, *Desire in L.A.*
Aleda Shirley, *Chinese Architecture*
Susan Stewart, *The Hive*
Terese Svoboda, *All Aberration*
Arthur Vogelsang, *Twentieth Century Women*
Sidney Wade, *Empty Sleeves*